RE-AWAKENING INTUITION

*the pathway of the
extraordinary life*

Angela Airey, M.NLP, RM, nd

LIFESTYLE DOCs
www.lifestyle.ca

Published in 2001 by
LIFESTYLE DOCs
Ottawa, ON, Canada

First Printing September 2000

Canadian Cataloguing in Publication Data
Airey, Angela, 1955—RE-AWAKENING INTUITION:
the pathway of the extraordinary life

ISBN 0-9687113-1-6

1. Intuition. I. Title.
BF315.5.A38 2001   153.4'4   C2001-901061-3

The information in this book is not intended as a substitute for business or psychological counseling. The author and publisher disclaim any responsibility or liability resulting from actions advocated or discussed in this book.

In the interest of preserving client confidentiality, all client names and, in some cases, identifying characteristics have been changed. The scenarios, situations, and results are real.

Copy Editing by Nedra Nash and Sheila Mather
Cover design by Darlene Thompson

Printed in Canada
Tri-Graphic Printing

To Denis,
K.M. and Greg

CONTENTS

Recommended reading is included within each chapter

There is no such thing as a happy marriage
but there is such a thing as two happy people
who happen to be married.

– Author unknown

PREFACE

My world continues as a joyful experience daily. It wasn't always this way. Like many of us, I'd been caught in the eddies of the river of life, pushed out from the center flow. Dumped, really, from relationships that meant the world to me, shunted from jobs that energized me and gave me status and confidence. I finally saw a pattern . . . and it scared me.

I've been re-awakened – through intuition – and now know that each of us passes through stages, gets stuck playing the same sad songs. Or, we can keep moving upward and onward to new and better stages of our lives. I was determined never to succumb to bitterness and aging I saw around me – in good people who had been carelessly pushed out of the temporary nests our culture provides.

Intuition is our basest instinct. It's what the hunted used to avoid persecution. It is our fundamental protection against danger. Safety is what Maslow says we need before any of the other elements can fall into place. I agree. Intuition can bring safety into our world. And, that's only the beginning.

Once re-awakened, your intuition will guide you to a peaceful foundation from which you can discover an invigorating, enjoyable and meaningful life. This life is yours, distinctly yours, personally yours, totally yours. Would you like to be delighted by who you really are?

Intuition is where you start and it will guide you, gently, at your own pace. It grows as you choose to grow.

Out of a place of despair, I have found a warm and safe centre that no one can ever take from me. I've found wisdom and freedom – that grew from tapping into intuition more and more. Then, I experienced fun. I was very surprised because I've always been serious.

This re-awakening unfolded naturally and easily in the steps I have outlined in this book. I have since taught many people in classes, seminars, radio programs, and on the Internet. Often, my students become dear friends.

Students have made qualitative differences in their lives. These differences are unique to each person and it's endlessly fascinating to see the numerous ways that intuition can manifest itself in people and the world. Remarkably, I have noticed that there is always a burbling happiness. It's as if when you find yourself, you celebrate from every cell, and it's joyous.

Intuition is not just about being introduced to the person you are, it is about becoming introduced to the best part of humanity and our natural world. A fully awakened intuition is your guardian, your protection and becomes your most trusted friend. "Alone" never feels "alone" again. You dance because you want to. You reach out and make friends because you know you have something to offer and receive.

The details and funny stories you will find within the pages of each chapter have been the lessons of my learning. I recommend that as your own lessons unfold, you write a book also. I assure you that your life will be worth writing about as you re-awaken your intuition.

God bless,
Angela Airey

ACKNOWLEDGEMENTS

I would like to thank my students, clients, and associates. In particular, thank you to those of you who have given me valuable feedback that has allowed me to edit unnecessary exercises and elaborate on important areas. To Keith, Mary-Anne Yolkowskie and Judith Birtwistle (a co-teacher), many thanks.

I would like to express gratitude to someone I have never met, but whose subtle resonating influence I have felt over many years, Susan Seddon Boulet. Her breathtaking and detailed paintings depict the numerous layers that make up who we are. Among her fine books are *The Goddess Paintings and Shaman.*

Thank you to Nedra Nash for her selfless editing and long drives to deliver the reformed drafts.

My publishing mentor is Sheila Mather of Mather Publications & Designs, Inc. If you are thinking about publishing and want someone to encourage you through the entire process, she is the angel of publishing.

I am grateful for two profound teachers: Denis Chagnon and Rolande – soon to be Chagnon, I'm hoping. Their example of dedication to healing and gentleness and humour and patience and support continue to guide me in my own quest.

My daughter, without whose love and teachings I could never have achieved the happiness I have found in life, remains my greatest joy.

Mr. Wonderful is Randy Jago.

Over two years my Mastermind Group offered continuing compassion and sensitivity as I grew through a series of difficult situations. To unburden yourself to a group of loving people who never criticize, but who offer insight and collaboration along with huge bursts of laughter, great food and glorious company at magical places like Constance Bay is a pleasure we could all do with in life. Thank you Rhona, Wendy, Jean, Nedra, Bev, Aud and Gita - you treasured my soul.

I offer the Mastermind tenets as an addendum. Thanks to Jack Boland. (I wish I knew more about him.)

INTRODUCTION

If you don't realize you're intuitive – and would like to be – this basic workbook is for you. Many of us read the body language of others everyday, but not our own. I'll teach you to read your own body's dialect, and it's really quite easy – once you know how. It will take some effort on your part, but together we'll get there.

My background is in Energy Medicine, a field few people know about. Energy Medicine complements traditional Western Medicine, and is seen by many as the missing component in healing. Energy Medicine works through what the ancient people called the meridians (they trace the path of the life force, also known as your vital energy, through the body). Energy Medicine is successful only when two souls (yours and mine, the healer and the healee, or the teacher and the pupil) agree and work together to accomplish healing at a soul level.

When I began learning about intuition, I was where you may be today – not at all sure whether I was capable of intuiting anything. I can now assure you that we are all intuitive. We simply need to learn how: how to recognize our signals and how to interpret them. This challenge in learning how to intuit is created by virtue of the fact that each person is different. We each come from different backgrounds, teachings, or episodes of fear, frustration and joy. We all have unique intuition trigger sensations that play a significant role in our own inner body language.

The first step is learning this new language called *Intuition*. It's similar to learning any other language. Begin to pay *attention*, *listen*, and *repeat*. You'll find that as you practice these three exercises, they'll become natural extensions of who you are, and you'll do them without realizing it.

Pay attention
Pay *attention* to the emotions that surface as you learn about intuition. In other words, discover yourself as you improve your natural intuitive talents. Also, note how you feel about your attempts, your misinterpretations, and your successes.

Listen
Listening includes just sitting or walking with an empty mind (having banished mind chatter). Spend time just *being* – with no agenda. From this point on, you'll begin to hear. It's similar to a telephone call. You don't hear the words unless you pick up the receiver. *Being* prepares the receiver.

Repeat
By *repeating*, you give repeated effort to this practice. As you practice, you get better. (Hence, the adage: *practice makes perfect!*). I suggest that you build into your day – everyday – some quiet

time. You will then be able to notice anomalies in everyday interactions. Learning a new language is filled with the frustrations of not understanding words and meanings. Sometimes, a language rule isn't standard, and sometimes it feels stupid to repeat a particular sound. Intuiting has its frustrating moments as well.

You need to be clear of emotions – which create mind chatter – in order to be able to capture intuitive messages. Intuitive messages are so subtle and move so fast that you must develop the reflexes of a serious athlete! If you study any of their training methods, you will find that they start by clearing their emotional blocks in order to attend to focus.

The first and most important ground rule is: *to intuit you must remain an open channel*. To remain clear you must eliminate emotions that take over your thoughts. Emotions to eliminate include worry, fear, anger, revenge, and even love - if it preoccupies you with plans - they will block your channel. Emotions block your vision and prevent you from receiving messages. The official word for eliminating these inhibiting blocks of emotion is *grounding* (described in Chapter Two). Several grounding techniques exist, and you must pick one or develop one of your own. Practice it daily so that you can make headway in learning how to intuit. Try each grounding exercise in turn and decide on the one that feels right for you.

Our society revels in the negative. Unfortunately, we seem to bond with *woundology* or our *victimhood*. To intuit, you will need to break this habit. Once you learn to ground and then change focus, you will be amazed how this helps assist you in separating yourself from negative inclinations and emotions. After practicing your grounding exercise, you may naturally focus on the positive or notice something good. You may have to make a concerted effort at first. It'll get easier, I promise. Then, either congratulate yourself or tell yourself about something precious you are observing at that moment. For example, you may see the first red flower of the season or a special butterfly (a little something is fine).

Intuition, I have found, works rather like a radio signal as we sweep the band looking for our favourite station. That momentary wsht as we cross a station – that's as fast as our messages tend to come. It takes a fair amount of care and self-knowledge to attend to the deciphering. When you get going –it's so much fun.

Eventually, you will arrive at a plane of living that is almost playful. This is because you will have heaved off layers of stress as you gain time, avoided the same old mistakes, and deepened your friendship with yourself. If you practice the lessons in this book, I can confidently promise that the amount of joy in your life will increase and that you will be happier and healthier.

Note
Unless you plan on rereading the book from start to finish, I would recommend not skipping ahead but rather read each page, chapter, and practice! There are layers to this science and you might miss a pertinent piece of crucial information. Each chapter builds on the information from the previous one.

Then, once you complete each chapter, spend a few moments pondering on your reasons for proceeding. Ideally, you'll come to a good place, and be ready, willing and excited about moving forward. (Also, hopefully you have well-meaning intentions. Any other motivation is a recipe for serious harm ... to you. Intentionally hurting another by using misplaced intuiting will boomerang with compound interest. Please don't go there. What we give we get.)

Although this book is intended for a beginner, it moves very quickly to an advanced level. In order to develop your intuitive abilities to an advanced level, you must be disciplined and committed to doing the exercises termed "GROWwork" at the end of each chapter. If you don't work through these GROWwork exercises, don't bother to try those in the following chapter. You won't get it.

chapter 1

WHAT IS INTUITION?

Know thyself. What do you want? Setting intentions.
Start noticing. The gratitude component.

*K*now thyself.
Who are you? What gives you joy? What is the scariest thing someone could ask you to do? Why do you want to know about intuition? Very often, we search for – and find – these answers when we're young, but we don't update them. So, I'll ask you these questions today – and please don't tell me what you are used to saying. Bury the habitual responses. Take time to really delve into the heart of your answers to the following questions.

What do you want out of your life now?
I can show you how to give yourself what you want, and more. Are you sure you want all that you think you do? Great satisfaction comes from working hard to attain a goal. If you don't plan to search your soul for your answers and practice your exercises, give this book away. You'll waste your time flipping through it. In the case of intuition, there are no short cuts. This is work. The most valuable work you'll ever do because you will approach the world as your world afterwards. You'll understand the preciousness of your

relationships and how to be more yourself in them. Know what you want with certainty, understand the consequences, and come.

Setting intentions.
Setting your intention creates focus. It means there's a road map for your intuitive self to follow. Before you begin working on intuiting, make a statement of intention based on what you want to accomplish. Perhaps you will say, "I thank you God for the ability to feel intuition," or " Today I intend to intuit at least one person." Another example (to accept enhanced intuition) could be to say aloud and softly:

"I am OPEN to, EXPECT to receive, and will TRUST and
ACT UPON all INTUITIVE GUIDANCE."

If that example isn't right for you, you can create a statement that is. This is your language and your comfort level. This journey is for you.

Most women chuckle in recognition of the joke about "kissing a lot of frogs before finding 'your Prince'". To avoid this wait and inconvenience, you may simply implement "setting intentions" in a most pragmatic way. I do.

At a certain point when I felt ready to entertain a new man in my life, I carefully searched for something which encapsulated what I was wanting. I found this magical picture in a magazine of a man tenderly enfolding a woman in his embrace. My heart melted. I added a line I had seen elsewhere "Older you get, more deep the love you need." Le voilà. I hung this combination outside my bedroom door (you'll note that I am a very 'physical' person) and "set my intention" … "just like this, please". Two days later I was teaching at a conference at Queen's University in Kingston, Canada, when who should walk through the door and right up to me? The splitting image of the man in the picture. He stood about three feet from me and surveyed top to bottom and then back up again. "Yup", he says, "you're the woman I've been dreaming about." To make it even more spine tingly, on my fridge is a picture of the car I want, a BMW 323. Guess what he is driving? Well, we were off to a magnificent start. Until I discovered that he was married. Most men in this position will tell you they're in the process of untangling. Sorry. I don't want to be part of that. So, at this point, I added a "supplemental". "Just like this man and not married." Two days later, a man walked boldly into my office and asked me out to dinner. Mr. Perfect, not married. In this case, it took me about four seconds to fall wildly in love. My supplemental had become, "Just like this, not married and capable of being in love with me too!!!" The fun I've had...

Try to remember to set your intention before doing your GROWwork exercises.

Here's one of my first and most memorable experiences with intuition. I was seventeen and a new, naïve university student. While walking down a boulevard in Quebec City – after dark – I was reveling in the mellow warm evening air and the freedom of having no one to check in with. I felt like a citizen of the world, having chosen to come to this magnificent city to learn the language of love: French. Caught up in feeling relaxed and delighted with life, and thoroughly enjoying the steady hum of traffic and pretty city lights, I noticed something. A man was watching me from his rear view mirror. He was traveling about 70 kilometers per hour, so the image was just for a moment. But I knew this was trouble. Immediately my senses were primed. I took a sweeping assessment of my situation. The sidewalk was poorly lit. In another ten steps I would be walking in front of a twelve-foot high thick cedar hedge. The house behind it was in total darkness. There was an opening in the hedge in the middle of the property where the walkway led to the front door. Intuition told me that there was a rape in the making. I considered turning around and sprinting but knew that didn't make sense. I wouldn't be able to keep an eye on this man. I knew this was a serious situation. (You'll soon learn that intuition is a completely reliable.) By this point, everything was in slow motion (this is very important because it gives you a chance to review all your options). The man who had been watching me loped towards me with purpose and strength. I saw him gauge the distance to the opening in the hedge. I had picked up on this ahead of time. My options were limited. I had to trust. The traffic light changed and cars passed us. And I trusted. I ran through moving traffic – I don't recommend that you do this by the way – and the man stood at the curb, seemingly dumbfounded and frustrated. Cars kept moving and I kept running until he had no hope of catching up to me. Not one horn sounded, not one car had to swerve. Although it was dangerous, not for a moment did I doubt my safety. While catching my breath, I looked up and said thank you. I felt grateful.

The two key components to using intuition are paying attention when the message arrives and being grateful for it. I paid attention when my intuition spoke to me about the man and I was utterly grateful afterwards. When I say be grateful, I'm not suggesting a religious ceremony (although, if that is right for you – go for it), you can show your gratitude by just saying "thank you." And guess what? The more you say thank you after each message, the more messages you'll get.

How did I know that this man was trouble? you ask. It's one of the most important elements of intuition to understand. Intuition is illogical, brief, and arrives out of context. It's off topic, and most often, out of place. And it's fast. You have to be alert to catch the importance of its message. It takes purposeful will to move yourself out of reverie into attention mode. This is intuition speaking. The good news is that it happens naturally when you are relaxed and at ease.

Note: Unfortunately, when we're relaxed and happy, we're usually not motivated to jump to attention.

Start noticing.
Try this: the next time you're driving down the highway and in a fleeting moment, the tiniest thought of police speed trap enters your mind – capture that thought. Between you and where you are going, there's a police officer with speed trap equipment. Now, the benefit to placing value in your intuition is this: you didn't get caught! Unfortunately, for many of us, we need to suffer consequences before learning a valuable lesson. It's better – and cheaper – to be grateful rather than having the thought, dismissing it, and then be pulled over for a speeding ticket (of course, only if you were traveling at a speed above the limit). Afterward, you may think that you "had a feeling" that there was a speed trap. This is where intuition can be tricky, in the beginning. If you can be aware, you may just notice some of the signals such as the car that was ahead of you is now pulled over, or a police car moving in the opposite direction. You'll see something. I promise.

When you see your incoming messages take form – this is called receiving positive reinforcement – write it down or hold onto that thought. Then, express gratitude. The more you register these events, the more you'll notice, and the more you'll pay attention.

Reading a stranger exercise:
Let's start at the very beginning. Next time you meet a stranger, take a moment before you say something. Read whether this person is good or bad for you. As soon as somebody speaks, you've lost this valuable, untainted impression. Years of unconscious training have taught you to listen to voices and tones. Voices lie and tones can be staged. The energy you read cannot lie. It can be turned off or protected, but it cannot tell an untruth.

   This is how to read their energy:
   1) Stand squarely in front of that person
   2) Do not cross your arms over the front of your body
   3) Register any feelings

The first few times you try this, you may not notice any messages. The classic ones are warm and fuzzy feelings throughout your body core (your heart, your stomach, your sexual organs). This means *yes* or *good*. A cooling-feeling, a general discomfort and unease means be *cautious* or there might be a barrier to work through. A painful stab always means *absolutely not* or *bad*. Incidentally, pay attention to where the stab, pricks, or pokes arrive in your body. This offers reliable clues on why this person is bad for you. We'll get to that part later.

Because of our individual histories, very often intuition arrives through your body in a symbolic form that only you can decipher. If your yes is something other than a warm and fuzzy feeling, you'll only find out by always noticing your common responses and recording what you think they mean. Then, the pattern will become absolutely clear. Another common yes message shows itself as *shivers sweeping from the top of the head to the tips of the toes*. Each of us has an individual mode. Please don't pay any attention to what your friend gets, your individual language is designed to be the shortest form of communication for you.

Start honouring your body. It is the temple of the soul, and it deserves respect. If you have been thinking about an exercise program, do consider Kripalu Yoga. One of the components of this particular form of yoga is paying attention to your internal organs. If you didn't think you could do that either ... stay tuned.

Or try an exercise, which I have developed (I have years of ballet training) that I call *stacking your backbone*. Stand with your feet shoulder width apart, bend your knees, tuck in your bum, and raise your chin. This effectively pulls your vertebrae into direct alignment, one on top of the other. Stay in this comfortable position for about twenty seconds, then rest and give it another go. Feel through your system. If it feels like you are starting to make a physical connection to yourself, add it to your regime.

In summary, as Gary Zukav says in *The Seat of the Soul*, "the intuitive person has conscious access to compassionate and impersonal help in the analysis of his or her choices, their probable consequences, and in the exploration of the different parts of himself or herself."

The gratitude component.
Always say thank you at the end of your GROWwork. It's the funniest thing, whomever is in charge of sending us our intuitive messages really pays attention to manners. The more you are grateful, the more open you become. Being open here means being accessible to receiving messages. You have to open the door to receive the visitor.

Note: To intuit effectively, it is helpful to have a body that is well taken care of.

The practice of being alone with yourself and your body every day will assist you in being aware of what's normal for you and what is a message.

Very often, intuitives will progress further into healing work. This is because the energy (the transportation of information) of intuition is love, and it is powerful. If you have a strong sense of love and are not ashamed of it – welcome; you will do well.

If you come from a place other than love, these prerequisites are learnable and recommended. You cannot intuit when you are tipsy, strung out on caffeine, angry, resentful, or playing head games.

GROWwork:

1 Spend some time in joy every day.

2 This week, do the *reading a stranger* exercise from within this chapter. Sometimes, you'll find this to be directly opposed to what your brain is telling you. Trust your body. This requires concentration. There are reasons (to do with the other person, not you) that you may not capture any response, so don't be discouraged if you get a bland nothing. Keep trying.

Also, you can try to read a person from a telephone conversation. When your phone rings, before you pick up the receiver, feel and record what you get.

3 When you feel uncomfortable, you are reading energy (the quality of the life force energy of the individual in front of you). Pay attention.

4 You have to be ready for intuition to come in from what seems like left field. Note the slightest references … in the beginning, it is rarely what you expect, and this can be disconcerting. If you have a chance to write your impressions down, perhaps you'll discover them to be symbolic. You have the key to this meaning.

5 Be grateful for every twinge. It's how we begin.

6 Consider reading this book with someone you trust. Maybe you would like to make a contract with this person to be your intuition partner. All your contract does is lay out your commitment. How often will you read together? Will you call immediately after you intuit something regardless of the time of the day or night, or at the same time every day?

The purpose here is validation from someone who is watching – just to find your glory. Promise each other truth, honesty and to be truly proud of each other as each of you learns to express your intuitive selves.

7 In today's society, we don't seem to value commitment or our word. This is something you need to change in order to practice intuiting. (To start, give yourself a gracious 'out' if you consider yourself afraid to change, because you are giving your word when you promise.) There is power when we give our word – when we use it correctly. We must understand that our word means something, and that breaking our word is bad news (we'll get to that later too).

Recommended reading

The Psychic Pathway by Sonia Choquette, Crown Trade Paperbacks, 1995
Learned Optimism by Martin Seligman, Knopf, 1990

notes

_____

_____

_____

_____

_____

_____

_____

_____

_____

_____

_____

_____

chapter 2

THE MIND-BODY CONNECTION

Opening and closing. Protecting yourself. Grounding.
Earth connections, sacred spaces and building your own.

Note 1:

This chapter uses a term called *visualization,* which was first coined in the 1980's when little children who had cancer were taught to visualize Pacmen scurrying through their bodies and eating the cancer pockets. Using this mental technique in combination with traditional western medicine, they were able to beat the statistical odds and recover. Visualization is daydreaming in a more disciplined format.

Note 2:
This chapter is experiential. Plan on getting up and walking around a great deal in order to accomplish this next layer of understanding.

Intuitive messages come through you body. In effect, you are expanding your brain into your body. We know scientifically that every cell in your body holds its own DNA. DNA is a computer-like memory bank; your cellular memory. Cellular memory, which serious athletes and coaches count on in training, can be a reliable and useful tool for you as well. You will teach your body to alert your brain to messages and to hold the sense of these messages until your brain has had a chance to capture their essence and begin to decode them. You may find yourself tuning into your body more than you ever have before ... all the way into the bedroom (so have fun!).

This is the mind-body connection. When you're being true to yourself, you breath deeply. Use this as a test when you are unsure. Be aware of the general feeling in your body – all the time – until it becomes second nature. Consider taking a class in meditation to teach yourself the sensation of being at one.

Everyday, take a moment to pay attention to each emotion – annoyance, empathy, caring, love, or hate – as it surfaces. Recognize it, and then notice how the emotion affects your body. Ask yourself these questions: How does this emotion feel? Where do I feel it? Then, *ground* (exercise explanation later on in this chapter) it to release it from your system thereby preventing any blockages to intuition. This becomes the foundation for incorporating intuition.

Do not dwell on emotions whether they're good or bad. The ultimate goal is to be clear of interference so that you are in the mellow, open state in which intuitive messages gain easiest access to your attention. Appreciate each moment. Trust that each moment is special.

Opening and closing.
Opening and closing require formidable amounts of concentration. I suggest you drink a glass of water, bring in your favourite teddy bear and really breathe before starting. (You should be ahead of the game, trust-wise, if you have chosen to work regularly with a partner.) Standing opposite someone you like, no arm crossing, concentrate on opening your heart. Simply concentrate on the greatest, most loving feeling you have ever had for anybody, then focus on sharing and direct the feeling from your heart forward, using your mind.

This should feel like a *warm fuzzy* from the person sending as well as for the person receiving. This is called opening. Once you have accomplished this, try closing your heart. It should feel distinctly different and less than nothing at all. These are very powerful emotions and as such are the easiest to transmit and receive. If you break into tears, simply acknowledge *with gratitude* the powerful person that you are.

If you have difficulty in sharing these emotions, keep trying. You can make a stronger impression forming a group of people into a circle. One person, the receiver, stands in the middle. At a hand signal, the entire group sends the person in the middle, who has their eyes closed, and either "ONE" open or closed.

Then, finish this exercise with gratitude: a prayer of thanks or a confirmation hug; something which expresses the fact that you are okay and have not permanently lost something in this exchange. If you have, ask to have it returned or ask for the group to gift you with Love *at this moment*. It is important not to be drained of your personal energy. You should be sharing Universal Energy.

Universal Energy is accessible by everyone who is open and good hearted. As you gift energy in good faith, this energy should automatically be replaced. If this is not happening, you must stop at this point and sort out the reason.

Review your motivation again, and be absolutely honest with yourself. *If you do not have good intentions, you can damage yourself by depleting your personal energy reserves.* This is the precursor to illness.

Blocks are discussed at length in Chapter 8, but do not proceed beyond this point without eliminating present difficulties.

"Intuitive development means training your awareness to expand, and to receive more information from others – from astral planes and from God. It is in learning how to expand your consciousness that you'll better understand how your instrument of expression – your body – receives energy. It is the art of evolving your body into a highly sophisticated receiver of vibrations, thus giving you more accurate information to work with as you interact with others. It is training your mind to be open and receptive to the subtle planes of energy that constitute intuitive activity. It is living a life that communes with spirit, sees things rather than looks at things, and is open and responsive to the guidance of God at all times."
- *Sonia Choquette*

My dog went through the ice one frigid mid-winter day in Ottawa. It was minus twenty-five. Annie's front heavy, Weimaraner's are. So every time that she scratched her way forward, the ice would crack and break and she was back in up to her chin. No foothold, obviously, no way to propel her way forward. Single Moms have responsibilities. We're not supposed to take life-threatening chances. We don't, when we are comfortably aware of intuition. Once you work with it, your intuition will physically bar you from entering an unsafe zone. You will feel a barrier as strong as pushing through water, when you are being lovingly prevented from going somewhere. It is up to you then. We all have choice. This is what makes us human. We can choose to pay attention or we can choose not to. In this case, as I plummeted into the water, I was consciously aware that I was doing something in which I was "protected." From underneath, I hoisted my dog onto the shore. She bounded ahead and then turned to check on me. I scrambled half the way up the slope. The place was deserted. You tell me what fool is out walking at minus twenty-five – except for a dog lover? I had four blocks to run, soaking wet. It took me four hours wrapped in blankets to dare to trust myself to stand up. You may see my dog and I on my Web site, still happy, still walking. We avoid ice on our walks NOW – as a precaution.

Protecting yourself.
It is considered good protocol to protect yourself as you work with energy.

Choose from the following exercises:
1 Cup your hands on your lap. If you are able to visualize, see yourself in miniature in your hands. Imagine an egg-shaped white light surrounding you. That is a traditional exercise. As an individual, this may not suit you.

2 You may prefer to work with a photograph.

3 It may be easier for you to stand and feel a cylinder of white light build around you.

Whatever you chose as your personal protection, you must include the component of white light and you must sense the safety.

Grounding
The other safety mechanism I recommend as essential is this process is called grounding.

Review the exercises below and choose the one that fits.
1 When emotions plague you, go outside; go someplace where you feel connected to nature. If possible, stand directly on the earth. Our earth is extremely forgiving as you may have noticed. By standing on the earth, you are making a personal connection. You can release all your emotional responses into the earth. It's as simple as thinking it so. This is grounding.

2 Next time you feel frustrated, irritated or annoyed, stop everything and go outside. Find your spot of soil and stand there. Purposefully set your intention: "I do not have the time to be gummed up with this emotion. I forgive (and you must truly forgive with this action and these words) and release into the earth. Thank you." This is also grounding.

3 Imagine that you have roots that grow from the bottom of your feet into the earth. Imagine them deep in the earth. Imagine allowing your problem emotions to slide down to the end of your roots, welcomed by the earth. This is grounding.

4 Imagine a pyramid whose peak starts at your chest. Imagine the base at the centre of the earth. Imagine pushing your emotions into the pyramid and feeling them sink to the base. This is grounding as well.

5 A different method you may wish to try is the parable of the gift. It is often explained as *you* being *your gift* to God. It is only through you that God can feel how you feel, if you choose to feel. In other words, for God to experience this, it must happen through you. Isn't that neat? So, hug the sky and ground to the earth. You become the connection between Father Sky and Mother Earth. Literally. Go outside and hold your arms out to the sky. With your feet shoulder width apart, bend your knees. Call in the energy of the sky, feel it rumble through you into the earth.

Set your intention and just concentrate. Be patient. When your legs feel leaden, you are grounding. This heaviness is connecting you to the earth.

Consciously push accumulated emotion through your body into the earth to free up space within you, to open yourself more. You are part of the eco-system designed to work with it. You leave the ego out when you appreciate the greater connectedness of us all. Are you starting to appreciate the sacredness associated with intuition?

You are now en route to creating your sacred space. Try not to get caught up in any religious connotations. Sacred is related to respect for the greatness which each of us is composed of in relation to the bigger picture. Have you heard that ego is easing God out? Try to feel like a part of the solution and not the only person in the history of mankind to discover his or her innate powers. Make sure you remain humble or, I can assure you, you will lose the touch.

Earth connections, sacred spaces and building your own.
Take a walk outside now, and pay attention to what you are intuiting. Places have ordinary feelings, ominous feelings, magical twinklings, and much more. When you find a good place for you, look around. See if you can't find a pebble souvenir. Collect good pebbles in a basket, in your house, or your office.

As you feel more connected – actually a piece of the universe – there are many more discoveries awaiting you. Also, you will begin to feel more comfortable out of doors. By now, you may be wondering how trees breathe ... and maybe you have been touching petals with a new sense of wonder. Use this newfound pleasure to develop a sacred space for yourself. It could be as simple as a couple of stones in a pile on your bathroom counter, or as elaborate as a circle of rocks in your back garden, complete with wondrous nature finds from your walks.

Whatever works for you to remind yourself that you are a part of a wholesome whole. A new layer of rejuvenation and healing will unfold as you continue to walk this path of focus and attention.

GROWwork:

1 Whole body exercises. Try doubling up on your senses. Do the stacking your vertebrae exercise and add a deep breathing one simultaneously, for example. Extend your capabilities in creative ways.

2 Make love to someone you love . . . a lot. Feel inside and out. Touch with gentleness and tender strength. Do the open your heart exercise while you're at it. Notice the difference this makes, the qualities you can add.

3 Start each day by stepping outside. Acknowledge a new day. Greet the day. You're living on a newer, fuller level already. Sense this day. Smell the air. Feel the vibrations.

4 Include grounding as diligently as you brush your teeth. It is the most essential practice for intuitive health.

Recommended Reading:

The Heart's Code by Paul Pearsall, Broadway, 1999
Awakening Intuition by Mona Lisa Schulz, Harmony Books, 1998

chapter 3

YOUR LANGUAGE TRANSLATOR

How are your intuitive messages coming in?
Kinesiology. Cellular memory. Cutting the bull.

At this point you should be grasping lots of intuitive information. You should be registering patterns and starting to decipher nuances. Does your intuition have a sense of humour? Mine does, and that's because I tend to get too intense, too concerned about missing something and this forces me to stop, laugh, and mellow out. My intuition feels very much like a partnership to me.

How are your intuitive messages coming in?
What is the language that you speak to yourself? Your guidance will be incorporating your very personal belief systems and your individual family history. If your father admonished you for letting out a family secret by yanking your arm, you may find an aching shoulder becomes your signal for breaking your word.

It's also highly intelligent. Complex explanations arrive in symbolic pictures, often in separate pieces that you'll need to add together. Understand that there is an interpretative role that you must become aware of if you wish to keep expanding your language base. You must develop a new skill – that of picking the essence out of the language of pictures. This is shorthand and it is intensely personal. No one will have exactly the same match of pictures or concepts as yours. For example, try this semi-tough concept. Create a quick cartoon-like image for *learning disability, release, and get over it.* And remember, there's no right symbol, simply one that has meaning for you.

Here is a playful method to prepare you for what you're about to learn. Once you work through the list below, you will continue to sense the qualities of everything you encounter in your everyday life. Again, let the symbol come to your mind and it will be perfectly right and personal to you.

If you have an intuition partner, they can read the following words to you, allowing you whatever time you need to develop a sense illustration. Or, you can do it yourself, as long as you include self-discipline. Try not to get side tracked. The more you practice, the better you'll get, and the easier it will be to work with your intuition. In a short time, you'll capture the message flashes, and feel more confident about what they're conveying to you. Soon, you'll be able to hold them in your mind – as a picture – while you take the time to interpret the message.

Exercise to intuit the picture:

Delirium

Hopelessness

Satisfaction

Honesty

Peace

Exercise to intuit the sound:

Diversity

Learning

Pre-supposing

Sun tanning

Gardening

Exercise to intuit the smell:

Joy

Vacillation

Helplessness

Indignation

Love

Exercise to intuit the taste:

Vacation

Swinging

Argument

Cure

Periphery

Exercise to intuit the feel:

Pomp

Clouds

Purple

Flag

Gift

Now, in any situation you should sense the feel of a place. I recommend that you take a good cleansing walk at this point. Ideally, you would go somewhere close to nature.

Where are your intuitive messages registering?
When you meet someone new, you may pick up a jab rather than a warm fuzzy. The jab is a warning. The part of your body and the side the jab affects is the key to the reason.

The following is a list of generalizations. You must learn to register and decipher where on your body your messages occur. One of my students feels either warm or cold on his forefingers and thumbs; for him, this means good or bad. Another special student feels good or bad in her thighs. The best way to do this is by using a method of note keeping.

1 Be aware of the foundation of all message sites. The left side of the body is generally feminine, the right side masculine. So, on a woman, something on the right side would most often refer to relationships with men. Refer to the side and the site when deciding what your messages are telling you.

2   Depending on how practiced you are at receiving messages, you could be *hearing* your own body's response or you could be picking up on someone else's. This is why systematic recording is so important. By listing and analyzing your messages, you will come to understand your own body's patterns. Once you know your own body and you get a new kind of message, you'll know instantly whether you are concentrating on somebody else's body language or whether this is a new message for you to pay attention to.

Learning the language of intuition takes extraordinary self-discipline and determination. In the beginning, this effort will tire you. Once you have good understanding of how your messages work, you will find yourself mellowing and relaxing. You will *double track* subconsciously. In other words, you will often see the humour in the translations and pay instant attention to warnings. All the while, you'll be carrying on with your life. *Double track-ing* is an added component of awareness. With this, you will have discovered the *being there* method of living. (This is a rare treat in the art of living.)

Also, I recommend that you try not to impose this view on others since they may become frustrated or nervous very quickly and withdraw. They may have a fearful response. If someone asks you – with genuine interest – about your intuiting development, you can lead him/her gently through, little by little, piece by piece

Message	Usual Meaning
Anal area	Fear of letting go
Ankles	Self-sabotage re: receiving pleasure
Arms	Look into your ability to embrace life
Back (across the shoulder blades)	Fear of giving or accepting love
Back (just above waist)	"Get off my back"
Back (hips and lower)	Money worries
Breast pain	Nurturing issues
Facial pimple	Angry thought, often against self (self-hurt)
Gut	Pay attention: this is serious
Hands	How you deal with experiences
Head	Invalidating the self
Heart area	How you give love
Hip area	Family issues need study
Knees	The inability to kneel to things. Inability to bend
Legs (calves)	Self-sabotage with regards to moving forward
Legs (shins)	Review "judgment", how you expect others to live up to your standards
Neck	Inability to look at issues from another's point of view. Stuck in your own perspective
Shoulders	Carrying other people's burdens
Stomach cramps	Fear. Trying to avoid change
Stomach rumbles	Changing beliefs
Throat hurts	Need to express yourself verbally or creatively
Toothache	Decisions to be made
Wrist	Self-sabotage by making things harder than they need to be

*Sources:
Awakening Intuition by Mona Lisa Schultz,
published by Harmony Books, 1999

Heal Your Body by Louise L. Hay,
published by Hay House,1984

Re-Awakening Intuition by Angela Airey, angela@lifestyle.ca

Consider carefully the parameters of each circumstance so that you don't jump to conclusions. The science of knowing happens slowly.

If you are ready for more, you can jump to the next level of intuition. Instead of just being on the receiving end, you can now begin to ask for solutions. Just be careful to have only one question on the go at a time. Answers often come synchronistically in pieces, and from different people. As Caroline Myss says, *connect the dots.* As messages and answers come, refer to your question. It's helpful if you write your questions down because the answers can come before you've finished forming the question (which can be disconcerting). Or, your answer may come several days later.

Try not to be too afraid or intimidated to ask for what you want. Play with a question. *What would you like answered? What would you like the answer to be? What is the funniest way it could arrive?*

Here's one of the first questions I asked openly and expectantly to my intuition. A while ago I had to buy a present for a wonderful woman I had been working with. She honoured me daily. Amidst a whirlwind workday, she would stop everything to ask for my input before pressing forward. Then, she would thank me for my response – every day, regardless of her workload. No one else in our organization gave me credit for my work or input. This was surprising since my job position required me to form the basis for project management and budgetary analyses for large, important board meetings. I felt invisible, and I was hurt and confused by this. Yet, this woman had a way of making me feel valued and respected. So, when I decided to leave this company, I knew I had to thank her in a very special way.

At that time, I was balancing a hectic work and family life and had little time to shop. One night after work, I settled into my car and thanked God for the reassuring presence of this woman. Then, I asked for help in finding something appropriately magical to represent my soul-felt gratitude. I trusted that I would be shown what I needed. Nothing in particular came to mind immediately. My usual route home took me past a huge shopping centre. As I was about to take that turn-off, assuming that to be my destination, a soft breeze of a notion brushed my temple. Continue to the next plaza. This was much further down the road, but I was absolutely certain. I followed the message and parked at the next plaza's parking lot. I knew I was doing the right thing. I was not familiar with the layout of this huge, multi-story mall. As I headed toward the closest door, I turned and was looking for an informational map. As the first boutique came into view, I saw my prize: a life-size photograph of a wolf, peering boldly around a tree. It was the perfect gift for this woman – she was a nature lover and particularly enthralled with wolves. A shiver gilded my spine. I had my confirmation.

Okay, here's flow in action. Not only was her gift easy to find, but also instead of being costly framed art, it was laminated; a much cheaper process and well within my budget! What's more, it was on sale!

Kinesiology. Cellular memory.
Asking questions in sincerity requires a big statement of faith. Sometimes, that's difficult for us to do – right away. So, let me suggest an interim technique called *Kinesiology* or muscle testing. It works

and is a little closer to our body's role in cellular memory. Do you remember my analogy about the serious athlete? They visualize themselves running through a game or a course, and their physical body reacts as though they were actually doing it. They were building cellular memory. Hopefully, by now you have a growing admiration for your body and its capabilities, and feel ready to try this extension.

Do you know about muscle testing? If you're working with a partner, stand facing each other. One of you will hold your arm out and make a fist with that hand. The other will ask a question that has an obvious yes answer. For example, you can say, "Are you 35 years old?" (If you are 35.) Then, the person asking the question applies pressure to the top of the fist and the person answering tries to resist this pressure. A *yes* answer is when the arm holds firmly in place when you press down on it. A *no* is when the arm drops gracelessly to their side. Also, your answers could be the reverse. Always check. When your partner is male, he will probably be able to push your arm down with ease. So, I recommend to men that they apply less pressure. Make sure you follow your own *yes* and *no*. Test for *yes* and *no* first. Once you establish your *yes* and *no*, you can get creative. You'll be amazed. Then again, this may not feel right to you at all.

If you feel comfortable with the concept, you can actually use muscle testing on yourself. Close the thumb and forefinger into a circle using your non-dominant hand. You pull through the circle using the thumb and forefinger of your dominant hand. A yes keeps your circle firmly closed. A no is when your circle opens allowing your dominant hand to slip to freedom. Once again, test to your satisfaction first. I know people who make major financial decisions this way. I have, in fact, confirmed marketing decisions with this test.

Cutting the bull.

Cut the bull. Learn to respond to every communication with honesty and integrity. This will help you to live in truth, a powerful platform builder for receiving intuition.

We live in a world filled with little white lies. We think we're protecting the feelings of others. This dulls our own inner sensitivity. To start, we need to develop a series of acceptable responses for social obligations that speak the truth without being offensive. When someone invites you out for lunch and you have absolutely no interest in spending any time with this person. How could you frame an honest and polite reply? Your partner wants money from your savings to go toward what he or she thinks is an extraordinarily important project. And your partner thinks it will benefit both of you. But you don't agree. So, you say ...

What you say matters to you and others.

GROWwork

1 Treat your "To Do" list differently this week. Instead of working through your list in the order of priority you've listed, work from the one that feels right. Then, move to the next one that feels right. You will be astonished at the amount you accomplish – and with ease. A sense of peace will set in. This is how working with intuition brings joy to your life. It gives you back your life.

2 Savour your saved time by doing something for yourself that you consider absolutely decadent (an afternoon snooze is my personal favourite).

3 What is your dream? Does it warm your soul? Are you afraid to share it because it's too sweet? Either write it down in private or share it in your sacred circle (group or person that you've been working with). Which component makes it so powerful for you? Make a milestone line (this is a calendar that uses events instead of dates as markers) and tuck it away in the back of a notebook. You may wish to share it with your intuition partner.

Recommended reading:

The Theft of the Spirit by Carl Hammerschlag, Simon and Schuster, 1992
Cracking the Intuition Code by Gail Ferguson, 1999

notes

_____

_____

_____

_____

_____

_____

_____

_____

_____

_____

_____

_____

chapter 4

FEELING WITH YOUR ENTIRE BODY

Feeling your inner organs. Illness.
Choosing health by forgiving and releasing through grounding

Consider how far you have come. You're now accessing information you may not have known about before you started. This next level of feeling inside your body is nothing more than a continuation of that process.

We're extending your senses into the deep tissues of your body. This is easiest to attain and works well in conjunction with a meditation or yoga program. Alternatively, working on your own presupposes patience. However, the methodology remains the same: listen, with focus.

Feeling your inner organs.
Begin with something easy. Bite into an apple or a popsicle. Savour the chunk on your tongue. Pay attention as your teeth break down the apple or ice to pulp. Taste again at the very back of your mouth. Then swallow. With all your concentration, listen to how your body accepts this nourishment. Sense, with the intention of

remembering later, where it is in your system. Feel all the way into your lower abdomen. Notice any discomfort.

In an hour or so, lie flat on the floor. Feel the path that your apple/popsicle took. Was your body pleased with this food? Were there any rough spots?

Still lying on the floor, following a few deep breaths, start at the very top of your head (or at your toes – your choice) and work through, very slowly, to the opposite end of your body. If you have the patience to sense your body, inch by inch, this would be beneficial. You will need a benchmark. The first time you complete the entire body scan, this becomes your benchmark for your physical body. Note any anomalies. They are not wrong, but rather your particular bumps and glitches. So, next time you scan through, welcome them.

Illness.
Anytime you sense a red glow or heat, be sensitive because this is anger on the loose. Hoarded anger is always the precursor to illness. You can stop the progression towards fully developed illness if you use self-control and open up your heart to forgiveness.

Sometimes – via meditation or visualization – you can determine the cause of a specific ache or pain. That process can be rather time consuming. With the exercises in this book, if you practice them diligently, you ought be able to live your life with no more episodes of ill health.

This is not to say that you can repudiate all medical intervention. There are occasions when it is sensible to rely on the advise of a medical practitioner. You need to visit your doctor if you sense any alarm or message as you scan.

We know that the liver harbours rage and the throat reveals a need to communicate. If you wish a comprehensive reference book on these relationships, consult Louise Hay's *Heal Your Body*, published by Hay House Inc., 1988.

Once you learn to pay attention, you can thwart colds, coughs, flu bugs, and more by intuiting the early weakness in your system. Scan your body slowly, relaxing each part with care and love. When you reach the troubled spot, you have two options:

1   Know that there are spaces between cells. With concentration, you can enlarge the spaces and allow the dis-ease to flow casually out of your system and off into the universe.

2   You can relax this location – totally. Not just for thirty seconds. Stop everything. Switch off the computer, television, or oven. Drop whatever you're doing and lie down. If you pamper your body now, and spend the time finding the emotion that is causing the block and deal with it, no physical disease will develop.

In order to maintain perfect health, when you note a precursor to disease – the stuck emotion – you can consciously relax that part until there is a free flow of energy again. With practice, you'll feel the energy flow.

The key here is to find the dis-ease early. We will eventually value our health to the point that when we feel the potential for illness, we will stop everything and focus on relaxing. It's not easy at first, but with practice you get better and better at it. It may even seem indulgent, but you'll soon find that you have much more time and energy by not being sick. You may wonder why you didn't think of this before.

Choosing health by forgiving and releasing through grounding.
Stuck emotions cause blocks and strains to the physical body by
siphoning energy – much like a black hole in space. From this stage,
the stakes rise as anger becomes more ingrained (which develops
when you don't deal with a problem). Anger and its affiliates:
rage, distrust, bitterness, and regret, roost and rot in your body if
you cannot release them. These turn into full-blown physical
disease.

There are many grounding techniques in this book. Pick one that
works for you and practice it conscientiously.

Refer to the grounding exercises in Chapter Two. You can design your
own grounding exercise if you prefer. Feel for the telltale heaviness
in your legs to confirm that you are grounding your emotions.

Now you should also feel a free flow of energy as you scan your
body. This is the Universal Life Force or Love. It is the part of you that
keeps you alive. Treasure it, knowing it by feel. When it's in good
shape, it flows smoothly.

When there are trouble spots you will sense bumps or temperature
changes in your energy flow. When your heart is affected, you may
be caught up in emotional turmoil; bumps and eddies of hot or cold
air is the physical expression. When you're traumatized by troubled
emotions, the record goes round and round and round, playing the
same song. It's tiresome. You regurgitate the same whining over and
over and your energy gets muddled at the same time.

Let go of setting the record straight. It doesn't matter if you were right
thirty-five years ago! It matters that you are healthy today. You should
be more relaxed, focused, sleeping better, making wiser
decisions, listening more, communicating more effectively and

thinking clearly. You should be long past the stage of keeping a balance sheet, which means not leveling the playing field. And finally, tasting joy in new moments – if you're seriously studying and working this book.

If you are almost there, but have a frustrating glitch, understand that forgiveness gifts you with freedom. If you can't un-stick yourself simply with understanding or grounding, you may need to visit unfinished business with your bravery intact and research pad in hand.

To deal with unfinished business once and for all, start by setting a clear intention. Then, ask for guidance from your intuition. Is there a relationship or incident you need to rectify? What is your body telling you? Can you apologize? Can you demand a hearing? Can you accept forgiveness? Can you give sincere understanding? In each case, decide your comfort level, but honour yourself. You need to accomplish an eviction of harboured anger. Please consider this as serious and do what needs to be done. You could be saving your life.

There are two effective methodologies you can use if you must work alone.

1 Write through your feelings, your memories, guilt, and admonitions, and then burn the papers as you speak your forgiveness.

2 You can talk it through by playing both roles yourself, using two chairs seated opposite each other.

Your choice could always include talking it over with the other half of your unfinished business scenario.

Make sure the kleenex box is handy. If you are doing this right, tears will surface. Allow them to flow to completion, and then let it go. Case closed.

If you're struggling to find the offending incident, work backwards using the location of the block, and find the positional meaning (see Table in Chapter 3 for reference). If the place of the compression fails to trigger the specific memory, you can try regressive hypnosis, meditation, prayer, or fun things you do alone. Your body is your temple. It deserves your reverence and respect – now. You wouldn't drop a friend in need so don't drop yourself. Stay with the program. Work at it until you reach a resolution. This is very important. Stuck anger permeates healthy tissue. That's trouble. Instead, let it go.

Take the time to be spiritual. Acknowledge that you are part of an immense and magical universe. Reach up and touch the stars. Name one for you. Sprinkle stars across your ceiling. Believe in your connection to the universe.

Choose relationships with the earth that inspire you. I know a cinematographer who travels all over the world. The most enchanting decoration in his house is a row of clear bottles that span his mantelpiece. Each bottle contains sand from deserts and beaches across the world; he filled them each time he visited. Each bottle of sand is different in colour and texture. It's unique and beautiful.

Relax into the one-ness. Give yourself a chance to feel as though you belong anywhere.

Hug a tree. When this was first suggested to me, I baulked. You're kidding, I asked this person, a medical doctor and a close, very credible personal friend. In response, he went out to find the most appropriate tree to hug. Older is better, he said firmly, wisely.

Here's how I learned about the wisdom of trees. Two days after a six-foot Japanese Lilac tree was delivered to my door, I decided to plant it. And here's what happened. The instructions were to dig a hole that was two and a half feet deep by three feet across. In the blazing sun, I started. I dug for what seemed like a long time — through stony soil. Hours later, hot and irritable, I thought the job was done, and quite well. Another few inches to even out the bottom and that would be it. The next shovel hit, clink and jarred my body forcefully. I had happened across a massive chunk of bedrock. Startled, frustrated and annoyed, I wondered aloud. Aren't tree roots supposed to be able to break through any rock in order to reach the water table? Nobody answered. I looked over at this bedraggled, obviously dry specimen of flowering tree. No indication there. I thundered across the hole and grabbed the trunk of the tree and spoke directly to the tree. "Do you want to get planted in that hole or not?" I gasped. A shot of electrical current sped down its trunk. My messages are often physical accompanied by a strong inner knowing. I knew the answer was yes. My tree still lives and thrives in that place today. I love to hug old trees – usually when it's dark outside. Not everyone will understand what I'm doing . . .

My Japanese Lilac tree has become one of my sacred bases. Next to my tree, I find the peacefulness I need to reflect when I'm working through a challenge. There, I ground, especially when I'm feeling resentful towards authority, politics, stupidity, and short sightedness. Beside my tree, I ask for help to strengthen my root system. (When I am upset I find it very hard to focus on building a root structure deep into the earth.) For me, that powerful tree is the answer. I recall the story of how this fledgling baby tree knew more than I and that seems to soften my "I'm always right" attitude just enough to allow me to lose the resentment and choose hope.

Remember:

1 Be humble.

2 Find your sacred space, outside and inside. Use intuitive sensing. Give the place love and feel the return.

Touching the earth with your bare feet (literally or figuratively) ought to be part of your everyday "To Do" list. So should spiritual and alone time. Don't get caught in a New Year's Resolution guilt. Instead of making a close-to-impossible commitment, when you're ready, you can begin by saying Just For Today, I feel intense glory. Just for today, I want to touch the earth. You can choose words that are right for you.

GROWwork

1 Meditate to find your guidance, if that's your style.

2 Body scan until you feel comfortable with your benchmark.

3 Revisit the grounding exercises to ensure that you're using the one that fits most closely with your nature and the one that feels like an extension of yourself.

Recommended Reading

Anatomy of the Spirit by Caroline Myss
Kripalu Yoga by Yogi Amrit Desai, Kripalu Publications, 1994

chapter 5

IMPLEMENTING INNER GUIDANCE

What does this mean for you? Double tracking.

*W*hat does this mean for you? How do you receive your intuitive messages? Do you hear, see, feel, or know them? How does it work for you most often? You may already be aware of when your messages reach you, and the easiest way. Do they arrive when you're in your sacred space, in a mellow frame of mind, or at a particular time of day? Honour your preferences. Value them. Be grateful for understanding how and when you are most receptive.

Implementing your inner guidance.
Are you having fun asking for, learning about, and evaluating your answers? Are you enjoying the ease of your decision-making process? Are you now meeting the right people and avoiding the wrong people? Are you sleeping better? Are you patching up all old disagreements? Are you saving time? Are you laughing more? Feeling more like yourself? Okay, now go back to your notes of what you want from Chapter One.

Name your *Guidance Director* – the kind, all-knowing part of you that imparts intuition. Develop your intuitive strength in the area where you receive most of your messages. It could be in a body location, a sacred place, a mellow state, or a particular time frame. Make that into a space where you spend quality, peaceful time. Create a tiny stone circle, a symbol or an emblem in that place as a memorial to the power of your choice for you. If it is a state of being, try to picture it and create a permanent collage expressing exactly that state. Respect it. Feel gratitude for it. Keep it private, unless you choose to share it with your intuitive partner.

Keep in mind that every one of us is an individual with unique expressions of self.

As a working mom, what I need is time. Here's how I instigated the intuition element in my life. I'm open to instantaneous detours. They save time for me.

I was driving down the highway recently when I intuited a turn into a furniture store. I hadn't been to that store in years. Upon entering, I found myself staring at the exact whimsical wicker chair I had envisioned for my room that has a dark slate floor – a difficult match.

Make certain that you are incorporating every wish from your original list into each applicable exercise. This is your life, your intuition and it is there for you. Make sure that the flowering of your intuitive talent reflects you and makes you happy. If there is a missing component, then simply clarify it for yourself, and redo the exercises with your new focus. Intuition should feel like guidance from a wise part of yourself.

What does this mean for me?
One day, after saying my gratitude prayer, I realized I rarely went shopping. As a working mom, my time was precious. I also realized that when I needed something, my intuition takes me to the right store. This happens much like it did when I found my wicker chair. I don't worry anymore. I trust that when I need something, it will cross my path.

The whispers of intuitive thought happen anywhere, even in the supermarket. One day, I received the message of crackers. I had just bought several boxes of crackers so I thought, okay, this time my intuition is wrong. Nope. When I arrived home, I checked and, you guessed it, no crackers. Now, having or not having crackers is not an important issue, but I'm continually shown how accurate my intuitive messages are. Every time. And, even I don't listen to them all of the time.

That's the charm of intuition. It's our life. We still get to choose the way we want to live. Pay attention or not. Ask the question, or not. Abide with the bad person or not.

There will be times when it makes more sense to turn off your intuition. For me this happens in big groups because there's too much information coming in at once. I begin to speak really slowly to accommodate all the listening I'm doing and end up leaving the impression that I am mentally handicapped or terribly distracted. For a while I mumbled *menopause*, but then people started offering remedies and doctor's names and so I decided to switch off, knowing any intuitive alert would still get through.

Generally you can learn to live with your intuition on – similar to leaving your computer on sleep mode – and awaken for important incoming sizzle. This is *double tracking*.

Double tracking.
At a certain point, it will become clear that your intuition is working full-time on your behalf. You will be well versed with this phenomenon by the end of the book.

Double tracking is paying appropriate attention to messages when they arrive (knowing they are for your good) while living life normally.

It had taken seven long years to conceive and I'd known the minute that I had, contrary to the shaking heads of the medical staff. My pregnancy was idyllic. I had morning sickness for a total of one hour. I adored my obstetrician. It was time to deliver my baby. Something went horribly wrong in the delivery room. Already in the birth canal, my daughter's heart stopped. No time for a C-section. My dear doctor leaned close to me while avoiding my husband, and he looked deep into my eyes. I knew he was giving me His trust. "You have a choice," he said. "It's you or the baby, what do you want?" Without hesitation, I knew this baby was a gift and without the slightest panic, I said clearly, "the baby." He proceeded, swift and strong. Eighty-three stitches later, and a great deal of luck and expertise, I was put back together. Interestingly, I was not concerned.

Intuition is strongest between mother and child. A feeling of peace accompanies those intuitive messages. I knew everything would be all right. My shaken doctor wept at the end of my bed later. He said I was his favourite patient and he hadn't wanted or expected anything to go wrong. Unfortunately, he gave up his practice that day. I only wish now that I could have framed the words around the intuition that would have caressed and sustained his soul. I know now that he felt personally responsible for my pain and physical trauma. He wasn't. I have cherished every moment with my daughter, even through her trying teenage years; I know she was sent to earth to teach me. We have a remarkable closeness. I can be away from home all day and zip back into the house for thirty minutes to change before dashing out again. That's when she'll call to tell me that she loves me. I feel so fortunate. Trusting in my intuition has given me life's greatest gift: love.

Double tracking will come naturally for you when you have been doing the GROWwork exercises diligently and they have settled into your cellular memory. You can then mellow into regular living patterns knowing that you can be alerted and will notice. This is the effect you are reaching for. It's like sneezing when you have to.

GROWwork

1 To organize your space means to organize your mind. Take one cupboard in your home. Clean it out. Once it's tidy, take time to look at the area and congratulate yourself. Breathe in the sense of order, cleanliness, and purpose. Try another small project, as time permits. See if you can incorporate this habitually. Trade tidying jobs with a friend.

2 Consider a formal time bank project in your neighbourhood or group of friends. Everyone has an expertise, possibly several. When a member of the neighbourhood or group needs a service, s/he can give that service and their time is banked by the hour. They can request any other service that is equal to the time they gave and have it logged by the hour. For example, lawn mowing equals legal work. Everybody benefits, and this builds communities. Offer to become the bank ... if you want to.

3 When you come home to an empty house, stand still for a moment and connect with the sense around the building. For yourself and others, you can rectify an unpleasant sense, whether this be a cold

shiver or a drop in the pit of your stomach, by smudging using a white sage bundle (available on most Indian Reservations and in some health stores). Burn it slowly in each corner while praying: "All bad spirits may leave because this is my space now, it is intended to be used for good purposes." You can make your own prayer that resonates with you.

4 If you work with an intuitive partner, hold both of his or her hands without verbal communication. Close your eyes. Share a specific emotion.

5 If you work in a group, group-share an emotion by holding hands, one person starts and passes it along through a circle. Feel the power.

6 Learn to greet someone by stepping outside of convention and listening with your heart. Validate your intuition.

7 Close your ears and listen with your heart.

Recommended reading

Something you've been meaning to get to – you choose.

chapter 6

THE SPIRITUAL PART

How to recognize your soulmate family.
Choosing your values without judging others.
No headgames here.

Choose simply to give every person your undivided attention. Respect them; stop everything else and focus directly on them. When you're on the phone, are you washing or making a sandwich at the same time? Stop that. Be courteous and concentrate – totally – on the person your speaking with. This is the only way you will hear with your heart.

How to recognize your soulmate family.
During these times of being present, you can feel your heart respond. (This is often the key to building closer connections.) Some people will know you, and it's uncanny. You'll feel close with these people, without explanation. Reincarnation occurs in groups. So, your current partner might have been your child or cousin formerly. Pay attention to the present relationships – how they feel , and see if you can find some clues.

I met a man for the first time; he had yellow roses for me. I love yellow roses, and no other colour. The next time he appeared, he had champagne – it's my secret indulgence. Until then, no one knew I loved champagne because I was afraid of looking like a snob. We care for each other deeply, yet we can go months without interacting. The sense I have of our relationship is very different from any other. There's an inherent feeling of protection. I would walk on broken glass to assist him, and he would do the same. Our relationship is based on deep respect and understanding, without a physical relationship. Neither of us was drawn to the other sexually. This was right for us, yet quite unusual for a man and a woman.

Be aware of intuitive messages, apart from the messenger. This is how to begin to recognize deeper relationships. People who know you better than you know yourself might be a part of your own reincarnation group.

Creeping delays is the term airlines use for short flight delays. It began with a 30-minute, then a 60-minute, and finally, a 90-minute delay. Eventually, the local area curfew came and there was no option but to reschedule a next-day departure. Thankfully, I was at my home city airport. Still, I was cranky and tired. I didn't want to ask my daughter to get out of bed at 11 p.m. to pick me up and bring me back to the airport for 5:30 the next morning. I was frustrated knowing that I'd have to pay my guaranteed hotel reservation of 225 dollars at my point of destination. I wished I had cancelled it before the 6 p.m. deadline. To make matters worse, the coffee shops were closing. As I walked towards a phone, I stopped. I knew that I was meant to stay at the airport tonight, but the thought of sleeping in a public place was not the least bit appealing. So, I assumed that the lesson was humility. (Words to the wise: "Don't jump to conclusions about intuition" and "trust that intuition is always for your good.") I ambled around feeling frustrated. No logical place to sleep. "This is an airport, after all." I was now lecturing myself. Tired, I wandered into the bookstore. Dazed, I was searching the wall of bestsellers when I felt the most amazing energy behind me. My back warmed and glowed as though a tropical sun was pouring that golden haze through me. I awoke from my daze, stretched and languidly turned, half expecting to step onto a beach. There stood a man I felt I knew, grinning at me. Clearly shy, he was observing my reaction with intense interest. "Hello," he said. The accent was Australian. For almost six years, I had been dreaming about "Rob from Australia." I had wondered whether this dream was about the brother of a friend I vaguely knew – the only Rob from Australia I knew about. Yes, this was Rob. I was not feeling passion, but better. Like finding the other half of my soul. We talked all night. We didn't stop for a moment. And, it wasn't chatter; it was heart-felt, deep sharing. A catharsis for every anguish ever encountered. I loved this man, this stranger, in a way that left me believing in past lives. I knew everything about him. He knew everything about me. We were merely remembering. I recognized the sense of him, the energy. I could trust this man. I knew without doubt that this man is grace and integrity. There is an uncanny resemblance in our appearance. Meeting him became one of the most precious encounters of my life, second only to the arrival of my beloved daughter.

Look at how people look. Resemblances are often more synchronistic than happenstance. If an historical figure looks unbelievably like someone you know, investigate. Read about that person. Do they have similar habits or similar loves? Watch where your fascination takes you and relate that back to questions you have about yourself.

Driving on a vacation trip, I was in that mellow state. I was leaning back against the door with seat belt on loosely, my legs stretched along the seat, and my feet tucked up against my husband. I was mesmerized by the warmth and happiness I felt for this man, and by feeling so cozy and trusting. I *knew* that this feeling had been built from more than one lifetime. I felt incredibly comfortable with him. I could even anticipate many of his responses.

As I savoured this feeling, I found myself looking at a different man, one who was unmistakably the same person. Dressed in a frilly blouson and pressed up against the opposite side of a stagecoach, I recognized my now husband as a gay gentleman. It was a staggering realization to make considering his considerable hostility to the lesbian relationship of his present-day sister. In a certain way, it explained the force of his repugnance.

I wish I could have stayed longer with my vision, and learned more. As soon as the emotional sense of the moment changed, I was back in the speeding car. It was a long time before I mentioned this incident to my husband. Bringing it up at that moment would have probably caused an accident! Slowly, woven into lengthy discussions, I told him about my vision, and it seemed to really help him mollify his family distress.

Choosing your values without judging others.
This may be tough, but try to avoid showing others how to live their lives, especially since yours feels so improved. Don't interfere. As soon as you feel a twinge of superiority, you should know that this is a warning signal. You have chosen a life discipline, complete with ethics (we hope), which works for you. There is no assurance that your particular recipe is perfect for the next person, and it is a big mistake to try to give anyone the short cut, even out of kindness. You may be aching to offer them your short cut, but it may not be their lesson for their path.

When asked, of course, offer your perception, but never direct another without knowing the consequences as they may rebound, perhaps unhappily, back to you. The best action is to become your own person so that you can be an example for others. Attract, don't promote.

No head games here.
Head games are applied manipulation to enhance your own well-being. We can take decades to learn this chess-like play. Learn, instead, to live in the moment and to give without being distracted by the pay-off. Strategizing scenarios to your benefit distracts you from the magic of where you are right now. Every moment has a gift to offer you. If you are preoccupied, it is very likely that you will miss out on the candlelight and romance.

GROWwork

1 Consider the person you may have been in a former life. Speculate on the quality of your former being. During moments of replicated feelings you can slip through the dimensions to another time. Be courageous, instead of afraid. Witness and learn.

2 Be gentle to all strangers. You never know whom you may be encountering.

3 Call a person the instant the thought reaches you. They may have been thinking about you – at that very moment.

4 Use pictures, crayons, or magazine cutouts, and create a valid representation of yourself now and in the future.

Recommended reading:

Any book by Paul Ferrini
The Science of Mind by Ernest Holmes, G.P. Putman and Sons, 1938
Life's Companion by Christina Baldwin, Bantam Books, 1990.

notes

chapter 7

THE SHADOW SIDE

Fear. Resistance. Sabotage. Illness. Energy Vampires.
Relaxation, tranquility and protection.

There are two patterns in life: love and fear. In theory, it should be easy to choose love. However, it takes a lot of practice to reach the place of choosing love.

Fear.
Intuit the tension surrounding fear. Intuit the edge that surrounds fear, which is often a temperature drop or a withdrawal. Acknowledge the power of choice.

Pick something that scares you. Work with your intuitive partner. Fear is based on the unknown. You can build an ally with your fear. For example, you may purchase a stuffed, friendly snake from IKEA and it might be the first step to overcoming a fear of snakes.

Use the project management milestone concept. Instead of calendar dates, accomplishments can be checked off as you approach the final goal. Or, work backwards from your goal and lay out a step-by-step program, otherwise known as baby steps. Often, it's easier to feel capable of reaching a goal when you can see the smaller steps in-between. The end goal may seem daunting or unreachable. You can achieve what you believe you can achieve. Go for it. You can do it.

Work with your intuition by asking for the answers or explanations you need in order to understand and deal with your fear.

Don't, however, start asking questions until you are confident enough to work with the answers. Once you ask, the answers will keep coming, stronger and stronger, until you deal with those issues.

You can switch off, but you will be closing down all intuitive learning, and that would be unfortunate, considering how far you have come already.

Everyone is afraid of change. Fear permeates our lives from the first time our mom whips our hand away from the flame of a candle and yells, "no, you mustn't touch." We learn to fear. Over time, we stop experimenting and trusting and do only what we are told. Some of us never graduate to the adventure of life. In the book, *Feel the Fear and Do it Anyway*, the author suggests that you consider the worst possible eventuality, and once you understand that, you usually find it's not big enough to stand in your way. Having an intuition partner can help here too. Rarely is anyone else afraid of exactly what sets us a-shaking!

Resistance.
Resistance is often based on our fear of change. In this society, whining is accepted. Leaving our group of friends and family isn't. Here's the risk. You may lose some of the people you are closest to because you may change or grow away from them. This makes

developing yourself scary. Maybe the thought of making new friends isn't quite as comforting as your ready-made circle; they may substantiate all of your complaints.

Resistance does not want to let go of the strong ties that we have built over time. It is the fear of losing something we thought of as having value.

If you consider your life an adventure, it may help you to venture forward without the keen nip of feeling you are losing something in the exchange. Working with an intuitive partner will help you overcome resistance.

Sabotage.
Sabotage is insidious. Self-sabotage is likely at work when you repeat unhappy circumstances. Based on the fear of moving forward, we are unconsciously disrupting our progress in order to return to the devil we know. Courage is a quality you learn from intuition because you learn to trust your own resources. Please try not to get discouraged if you suspect self-sabotage. Recognizing the problem is half of the solution. Try to track when you self-sabotage – or are experiencing the same painful scenario – and devise small steps to release the block rather than taking a humungous leap.

To break your entrenched pattern of self-sabotage, try using the milestone concept outlined under *Fear* as shown above.

Illness.
Illness is your intuition's last resort to get you to notice something about yourself and the patterns you need to change to promote your own well-being. Always treat illness as a blessing. It's a gift of time to reflect. And it provides the perfect opportunity for you to do your homework! Illness is a serious message. I recommend that you pay attention.

Breast cancer, for example, has been documented as a message to nurture yourself. If you beat the cancer and don't start doing something powerfully rewarding for yourself, you'll be dealing with the occurrence of a further self-destructing illness.

Energy Vampires.
Energy Vampires are real. Quite unknowingly, some really nice-seeming people can suck you dry. Respect yourself enough to move out of their sphere immediately. We often know them as controllers and manipulators, and frequently, as mom or dad. Trust yourself. The hairs on the back of your neck never stand up for enjoyment. That deep sick feeling in the centre of your being: that's a warning. And be mindful of the fact that just because someone sucks your energy, it doesn't mean that he or she sucks your best friend's also. Energy dynamics are very individual. Your vulnerability might just be the perfect complement to this person. Don't judge. Just listen and learn.

Relaxation, tranquility, and protection.
The counterbalance to the dark side is an understanding and practice of relaxation, tranquility and protection. Relaxation charges up your batteries and keeps your intuitive senses on alert. Rest is not just a four letter word, it's a lifestyle pattern based on sense. Recuperate, eat, sustain your interests, and trust. Part of growing up and accepting responsibility for adulthood is accepting your own limitations. Build around them. Make them the centre of your personal ritual schedule. Enjoy them, for this is your body graciously teaching you about yourself.

Within moments of tranquility, you'll receive your best intuitive understandings. Relish them. See if you can bless yourself by arranging a fifteen-minute bubble of tranquility for yourself – once a day.

Protection works, but you must be aware of the danger in order to signal protection into place. Allow yourself to live consciously as a double tracker. Always trust your intuition. A body cannot lie. Review Chapter Two, on protection exercises, if these are not part of your everyday living patterns

GROWwork

1 Take the time to record the people who habitually suck your energy and determine gracious ways to drop them from your circle.

2 Note those people who bring in vitality, giggles and new ideas. Step forward. You are a vibrant, fun person. Offer friendship – it's the greatest pleasure there is.

3 Learn not to step forward to save people. They have their own choices. Act instead as an example. Value yourself as too important to waste.

4 No-one is perfect; if you catch yourself sliding, don't give up. Simply view this as a reminder (after all, you did catch yourself), and keep going. Life is learning.

5 Using pictures, crayons, magazine cutouts, and create a valid representation of yourself now and in the future.

6 Through Yoga, relax different parts of your body at will.

Recommended Reading

Any old journals or diaries you kept through tough times.

notes

chapter 8

SUCCESS!

From worry to life flow and managing all that extra time.
How to play with intuition. Continuing education.

The quality of your friends will change as you learn to value yourself and get away from whiners and complainers. This can seem daunting. Just take it slowly and enjoy the fact that every moment has precious meaning.

The change: from worry to life flow.
The closer you are to walking the spiritual path, the more your life will revolve around synchronicity and being *in the flow*. Your life should have a lighter feel to it, a trusting, an almost *waiting to see what the punch line will be* quality. This is not laziness; it's closer to detaching yourself from everyday traumas and witnessing the ebb and flow of life and its inherent humour and pleasure.

Let's take this chapter to evaluate what you have gained and to using this salvaged time – the time you've gained by using your intuition – to clarify your goals.

Using intuition in your everyday life along with the expertise you have gained through your GROWwork assignments, you should have greater confidence in making decisions, decisions that are right for you and based on your needs and wishes. At this point, you should not be experiencing *muddy waters* because of inappropriate suggestions by well-meaning people who don't live in your skin. Your personal relationships should be running better. Your work-based decisions should be more professional and less fraught with anxiety. Your financial decisions should be better metered. All in all, you should be spending far less time and effort making decisions.

Managing your life with all the time you have gained.
Step back and watch yourself. At the end of the day, rewind the tapes. You can work to improve your on-stage performance (your life in action). You can replay scenarios and try out different endings. Make your characters larger than life and allow them to live. Walk down different scenarios, you may be surprised to see how they might have played out.

You will be fascinated by the variety of choices you had on any given day. Perhaps in retrospect, the choices you made were curiously funny. Just remember, they were never wrong. They were right for the time you made them. Trust yourself. Respect the fact that you made choices and understand that nothing is forever. You may make different choices tomorrow. Each new day holds new opportunities.

The results of your choices become less punitive this way. The point becomes more about how you would have lived each day and the quality of the connections you made. You'll become more reflective and more forgiving of yourself.

In order to maintain this mellowed management of your life, you need a spiritual component that equals time alone. Don't shortchange yourself in this department. Honour your needs first. Consider it a preventative maintenance program, like servicing your car.

You need to do grounding exercises every day.

You need to be grateful. The practice of writing down five items for gratitude every day is a good one. Check the Addendum if you require a format. If you include gratitude thinking in each part of your day, and it is becoming a natural habit to be grateful, you may wish to stop writing it down and simply continue to live in that mode. Most of us get bogged down with unpleasantness from time to time. Then, we start journaling again and quickly revert to gratitude mode. It is such a nice way to live.

You need balance in your life. Balance is my personal equation for romance. I love kisses and hugs, snuggles, and whispered nuzzles. That's what brings me back to balance. So does repainting my kitchen. Find instances where you lose the concept of time because you are so immersed in the creative play. That's balance. For you, it may be hitting a golf ball, sewing curtains, or making a stew.

Now that your regular life is under control, you've gained time and a strong sense of well being. Does that sound like success to you? Successful people are drawn to successful people. Successful people consistently keep moving. They do things they want to do. Having tapped into the secret of success, you can too. What has your biggest dream been? Now expand it.

A new look.
As we get older, one of our most unfortunate losses is our child-like ability to play. It resurfaces sometimes when grandfathers get down on their knees to tag a delighted puppy or a little toddler. Sometimes, we are fortunate enough to come across a lover who melts and

moulds around our body as a vulnerable, young person rather than an equal determined to play the equality role. Who do we enjoy the most? People with a child-like wonder who aren't afraid to try different poises and poses to entertain or those behaving professionally. I remember fun and playful people with the greatest fondness.

It's not that far away for us. Thus far, we've broken lots of barriers that would normally keep us corralled in the crusty serious business of living. I've got you listening to tummy rumblings without the embarrassment that surrounds, "Oh, no, that's not supposed to happen in good company." I might even have you hugging trees!

How to play with intuition.
Stop and laugh. Intuition is the game of life. Play with it. Enjoy the magnitude of your life. Being special emanates outwards, raises the vibration of those around you in a ripple effect, and actually influences the state of the world.

It's like floating in a warm ocean. There's you and all these waves to caress your body. Waves can be annoying; they move you from where you are, directly lined up with your towel on the beach. Or, you can lie back with your ears underwater and feel a part of the swelling and sloping of the sea. You can tuck your toes into the sand and squish it between your toes or you can worry about scratching your perfect nail polish. You can silently swim up behind your lover and capture him or her in an underwater embrace or you can be nervous about your bathing suit becoming untied.

Play with your body. Enjoy it, express yourself through it, whether through the practice of Kundalini yoga or skate boarding. Source this joyful energy for yourself. Do what brings you joy. Try it all. Add to your life.

My God has a sense of humour. Too much in my life has been absolutely hilarious – in retrospect. So, as the receiver, I have learned not to dwell in the momentary pain or the embarrassing anguish of everyday situations. I save and savour the details of life's humbling set-ups to tell to those around me. My storytelling brings mirth and pleasure to my students and my close friends. Laughing with me, they frequently add gurgles of their own, funny similar episodes that leave us in happy giggles.

In business sometimes you have to put on a brave front. It was one of those occasions. I was uneasy when I arrived at the Newark airport, but strode over to the information counter as if this was any other day. The worker told me I could get to downtown Manhattan from here and that eleven US dollars will get you the ticket. Then, if I walked across the street I could catch the bus.

Still a little wobbly with nervousness, I stepped out into the bright sunshine and crossed the street. In the stall, already waiting was one of those luxurious long distance buses. Okay, as soon as I am sitting in my seat, I'll feel better, I said to myself. I have one of those under-the-seat pull bags and navigating curbs can be a little tedious, not to mention embarrassing when everything tips over. Concentrating very hard on looking natural (aren't we all crazy sometimes?), I arrived at the bottom boarding step of the bus. The biggest effort of concentration was now over and so I heaved a sigh of relief as I turned to push the long steel handle into place before lifting and carrying my bag those three steps up onto the bus and … there stood the most elegantly handsome man I have ever laid eyes on. You know how they say that time stops? It does. I gazed into the deepest, most wondrously sexy eyes that I have ever come across and heard my voice [MY voice!] say, "YOU must be the person I have come to New York to meet". The rest, as they say, is history.

Lightening up.

By removing the excess burdens that weight us down (for example, concern over how we'll look while describing some eccentric moment), we gain an ability to walk taller, and to lighten up. A sense of fun expands with your growing senses. You'll find a secondary effect of intuiting is an enjoyment in just the breath of the air, the touch of the sun, the panoramic smell of the woods, and the deep warmth of a hug. You will pay attention to clouds as they flow, marvel at their speed and ever-changing shapes, and realize their affect on our earth. You will notice strangers, cherish their quirkiness, and blend their flavour into your stories. The fun extends into other dimensions, cackling over the misunderstanding of totally obvious messages.

Deadlines become milestones, and where is the harm? Changing your vocabulary changes a lot. Changing your emphasis from irritable to playful brings far quicker resolutions. You feel more generous in the process.

Lightening up includes traveling. Just pick up and go. Carry on baggage only. Would that be lightening up for you?

Continuing education.

In life, you can learn something for every moment you pay attention. I met an aboriginal Healer once who told me she'd learned everything she knows just by watching wild animals.

If you are shy about talking to people at a bus stop, lean back and study and learn. Do the same thing when you're in a line-up. Feel your body make assessments. Notice how time can fluctuate and bend.

Responsibilities to yourself.
Make yourself a responsibility, your number one priority.

My favourite quote goes something like "If you think you are too small to be effective, you've never been in bed with a mosquito." I have come to believe that we as individuals can affect world thinking by how we live our lives on a daily basis.

GROWwork

1 Write a postcard to yourself today. Why are you proud of yourself regarding your intuition practices? Why are you proud of yourself regarding your decision-making practices? Think back over the process of decision-making over your lifetime. Enjoy your new skills. Find a way to mail it to yourself six months from now.

2 Think of your body as your friend. Spend time treating your friend.

3 Remember what it was that you wanted to become when you grew up. What qualities were you striving to attain? Is there any of that magic left that you could transfer to a current desire?

4 What are you most grateful for? Write down things about yourself such as who you are, and how you think, feel, see, hear and intuit?

5 Can you describe this gratitude to a child in a mythical tale or drawing?

6 Could you add a Christmas or household decoration to your personal collection that is purely whimsical but representative of your inner work?

7 Select a binder. Name it "Dreams Becoming Reality." Start collecting ideas that you will put into practice, design, or create.

8 Play with the idea that you can accomplish your expanded dream. How could you? When do you start? In life, there should be no ordinary moments.

9 Your legacy to mankind – what would you like it to be? The collective subconscious will capture it anyway; you don't have to worry about how to pass it along. I'm referring to the quality of your legacy.

Recommended reading

Go to the library and stand in front of the autobiography section. Run your hand slowly across the spines of the books. Feel for warmth or cold, a definite change in temperature or a whispered movement of air. Choose that autobiography to read; it is meant for you.

chapter 9

YOUR NOTES

The certification process.

Your own notes should form the backbone of your understanding of intuition because intuiting is a personal science. Keep them in a sacred place.

For certification, please send all GROWwork assignments answers to:

Angela Airey, M.NLP, RM, nd
President, LIFESTYLE DOCs
SENTOSA, 11 Briarcliffe Drive, Ottawa, ON K1J 6E3 Canada
E-mail your answers to: **angela@lifestyle.ca**
(Also, you can visit our Web site at **www.lifestyle.ca** to receive an intuition tip of the week!)

Providing your understanding is satisfactory, you will receive your certificate in the mail within six to eight weeks.

I'd like to close with a summary from Sonia Choquette.

The *intuitive* pathway is the pathway of learning how to express our highest degree of creativity and love in this lifetime. It is the pathway of living life receptive to spiritual assistance and conscious of all the planes of energy we share with each other, with higher planes and with God. The *intuitive* pathway is not the usual pathway so many follow, focused on the ego, feeling alone and frightened by others. It is a spiritual pathway focused on connection to God, on our creative purpose and on spiritual growth. It is the pathway of the extraordinary life.

If you walk the *intuitive* pathway, you live in the world differently from the ordinary person. You look at life differently and respond to it differently. You know that you will be helped with each experience you face, however difficult. It is the pathway of trust and belief. This is what we mean when we talk about intuitive ability.
- Sonia Choquette

My summary is that intuition gifts you a whole new world . . . your world.

Now, I'd like you to add your summary.

_____

_____

_____

_____

_____

_____

GROWwork

1 Keep in touch

2 Plant a tree

Recommended reading

Your course notes – from the beginning

Addendum 1

GRATITUDE
Journal template

MONDAY

1 _____

2 _____

3 _____

4 _____

5 _____

TUESDAY

1 _____

2 _____

3 _____

4 _____

5 _____

WEDNESDAY

1 _____

2 _____

3 _____

4 _____

5 _____

THURSDAY

1 _____

2 _____

3 _____

4 _____

5 _____

FRIDAY

1 _____

2 _____

3 _____

4 _____

5 _____

SATURDAY

1 _____

2 _____

3 _____

4 _____

5 _____

SUNDAY

1 _____

_____

2 _____

_____

3 _____

_____

4 _____

_____

5 _____

_____

Addendum 2

MASTERMINDING

We need other people to help us to bring out our true selves, to be totally successful, and to energize our outlook.

- No one mind is ever complete;
- With like minded people - the possibilities are endless;
- On purpose for something greater, grander than myself;
- Blend mind power in action to obtain unlimited results financially, corporately, entrepreneurially, psychologically, spiritually & familially;
- Work with us, support us, encourage us, empower us to fulfill our relationship with the Mastermind alliance - each other, ourselves & to a greater purpose;
- Positive mental attitude;
- Contribution.

GUIDELINES

1 Two to six individuals, maximum of twelve
2 Meet regularly - weekly if possible
3 Start the meeting by reading the Mastermind Principles
4 Share something positive that happened since the
   last meeting
5 Share problem/opportunity that was experienced since last
   meeting. Ask for the support you would like.
6 Members should be supported visually, verbally and from
   the heart.

DEDICATION AND COVENANT

I now have a covenant in which it is agreed that the Mastermind shall supply me with an abundance of all things necessary to live a success-filled and happy life. I dedicate myself to be of maximum service to God and my fellow human beings, to live in a manner that will set the highest example for others to follow and to remain an open channel of God's will. I go forth, with a spirit of enthusiasm, excitement and expectancy.

Jack Boland

MASTERMIND PRINCIPLES

1 I release myself to the Mastermind because I am stronger
   when I have others to help me.
2 I believe the combined intelligence of the Mastermind
   creates a wisdom far beyond my own.

3 I understand that I will more easily create positive results in my life when I am open to looking at myself and my problems/opportunities from another's point of view.

4 I decide to release my desires totally in trust to the Mastermind and I am open to accepting new possibilities.

5 I forgive myself for mistakes that I have made. I also forgive others who have hurt me in the past so I can move into the future with a clean slate.

6 I ask the Mastermind to hear what I really want: my goals, my dreams and my desires. I hear my Mastermind partners supporting me in my fulfillment.

7 I know, relax and accept, believing that the working power of the Mastermind will respond to my every need. I am grateful knowing this is so.

Next Level

ESTABLISHING INTUITION

Chakras are like diskettes with your programming on them. This means that you can discover what programs drive you and revise them to reflect the true you instead of old habits.

A healthy relationship. Shared intuitive messages (they come to the part of the couple easiest to reach but can be meant for either partner).

Trust.

About the Author

Angela Airey, also the author of Intuition – a Business Skill, works as a brief, solution-oriented therapist in a specialized field. Her seminars, workshops, and lectures on intuition draw people from around the globe – thanks to the World Wide Web. Her gentle nature and love of her work shines through in her speaking events on intuition. You can visit her Web site at http://www.lifestyle.ca for details about "Intuition Radio", a call-in show hosted by Angela.

Angela lives in Ontario, Canada with her Weimaraner dog, Egyptian Mau cat, and her precious mill house cat.

Angela and her group are also available for consulting through Harvesting Results Consulting Inc. at 1 (888) 598-4655.

photo: Kaylyn Mary Airey